Adult Coloring Book Designs

Mandalas to Relax and Enjoy

Leroy Vincent

All Rights reserved. No part of this book may be reproduced or used in any way or form or by any means whether electronic or mechanical, this means that you cannot record or photocopy any material ideas or tips that are provided in this book.

© 2016 Leroy Vincent

ISBN 978-1-60796-597-8

Published by Revival Waves of Glory Books & Publishing

PO Box 596| Litchfield, Illinois 62056 USA

www.revivalwavesofgloryministries.com

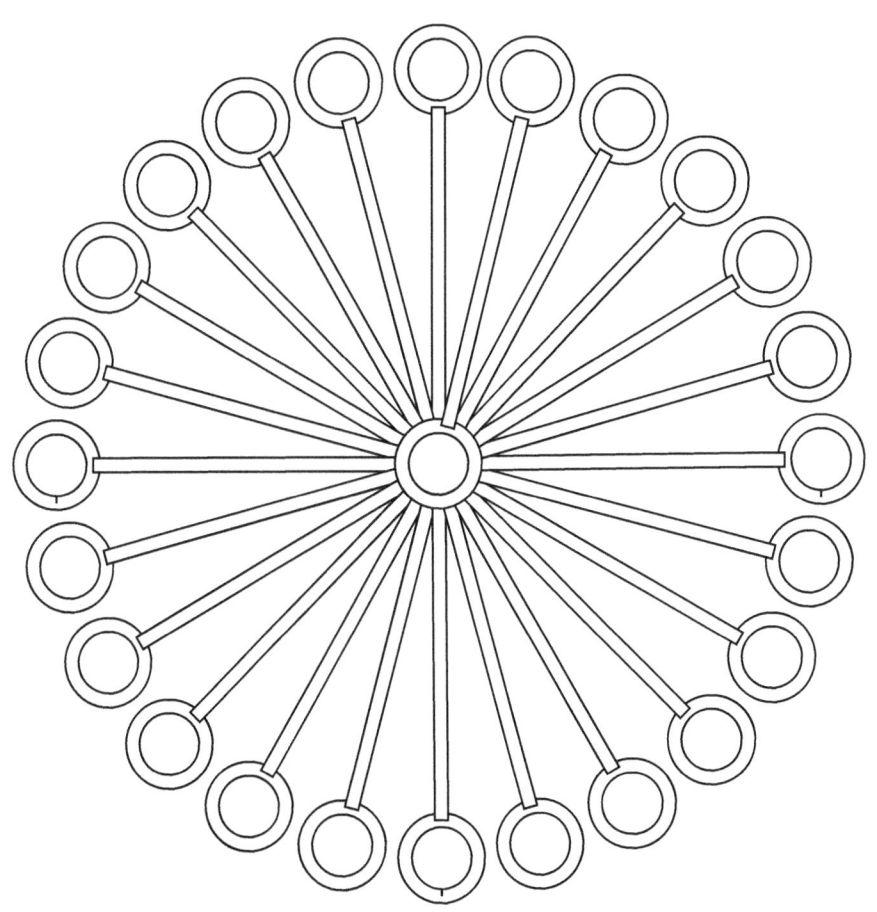

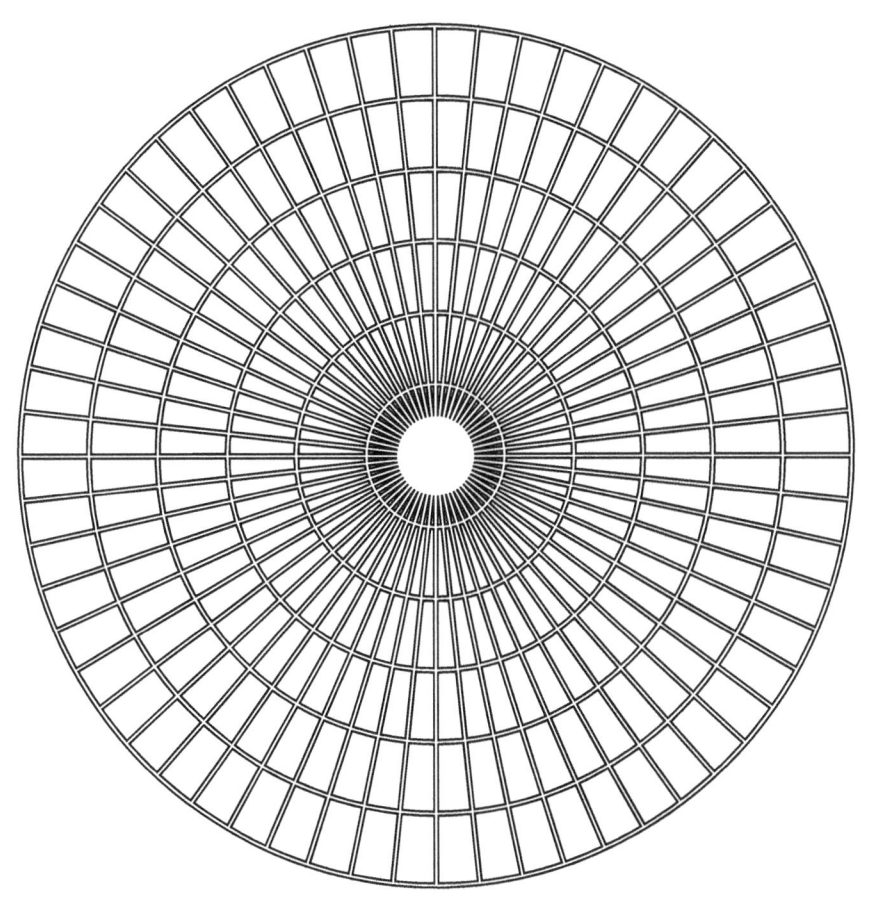

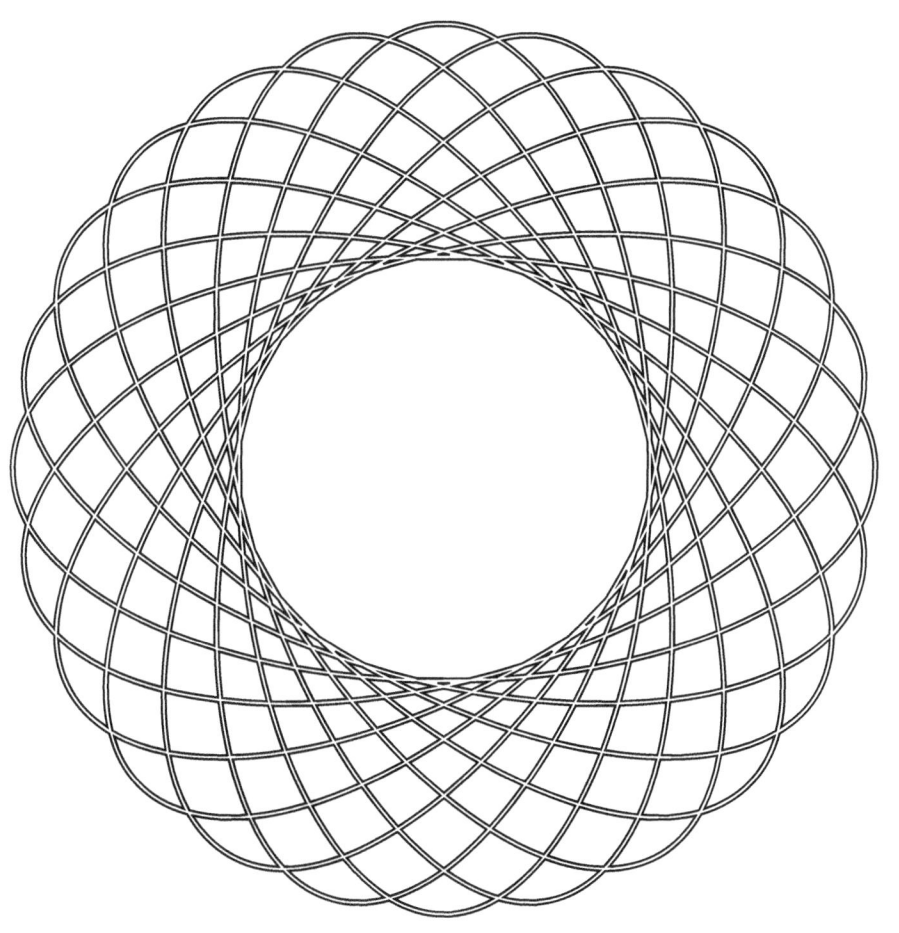

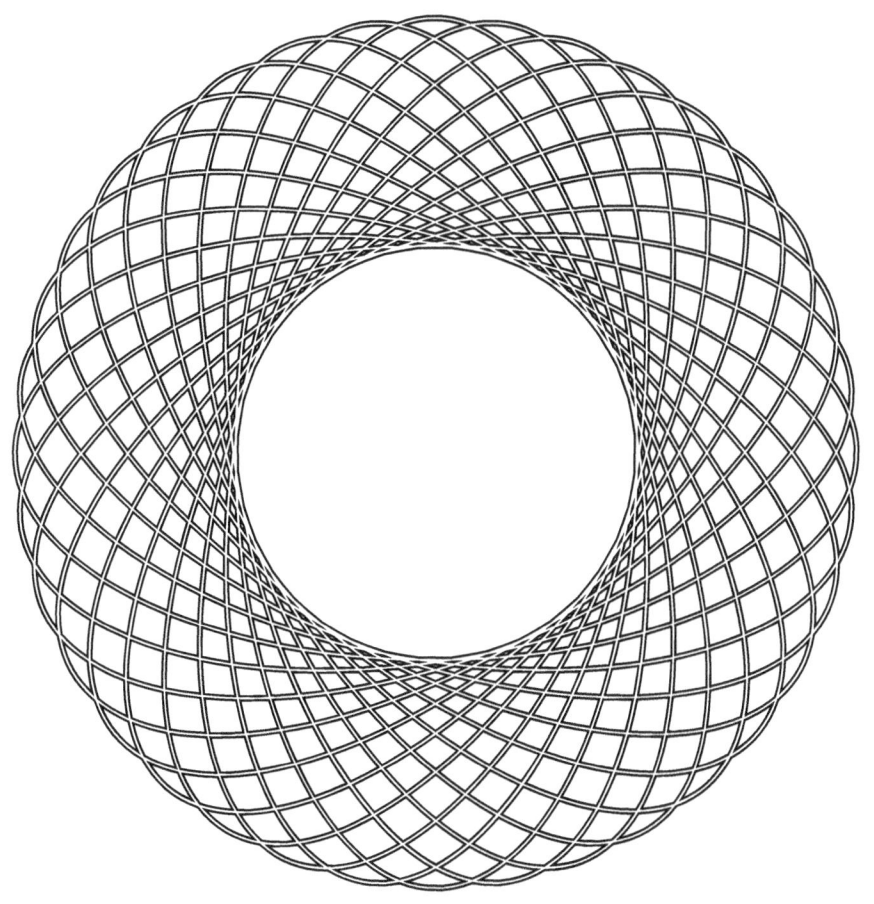

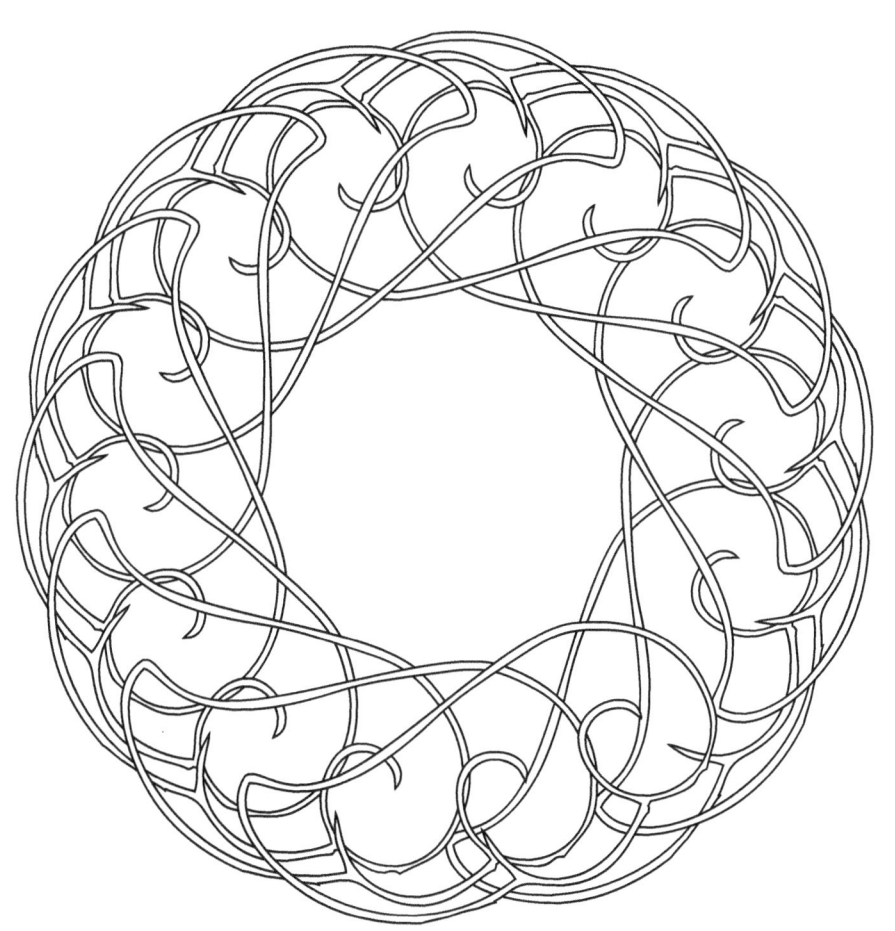

Also By Leroy Vincent

Mandala Coloring Books
(Book Series)

Adult Coloring Books
(Book Series)

Adult Coloring Book Designs
(Book Series)

www.ingramcontent.com/pod-product-compliance
Lightning Source LLC
Chambersburg PA
CBHW052029070526
44584CB00016B/1959